Touchdown

8 Key Factors to Score a Touchdown in Selling

D.N. Chadha, MA, BA Honors Author

ISBN: 1448612349
ISBN-13: 9781448612345

CONTENTS

ABOUT THE AUTHOR

D.N. Chadha has more than twenty years of invaluable experience in direct sales with established and start- up pharmaceutical companies, in addition to more than ten years of management experience in leading sales teams to success. As the regional sales director at a major Japanese pharmaceutical company and co-director of sales at a growing pharmaceutical company, he has successfully built and managed a sales force of more than 200 sales representatives that achieved corporate sales in excess of $150 million. While managing sales teams as a national sales manager with another start-up pharmaceutical firm, Mr. Chadha consistently exceeded revenue projections for the company. He has an enviable track record of success in both direct sales and coaching and managing sales teams that has delivered results and achieved corporate revenue goals over a period of thirty years. He has executed the eight key factors successfully by working in the trenches with his customers and sales representatives.

Mr. Chadha has a Master of Arts degree in English Literature and Bachelor of Arts (honors) degree from Delhi University in India. He has been trained in selling and sales management by the leading pharmaceutical companies, and has received several awards for his top sales performance both as an individual contributor and leading sales teams.

NOTES FROM THE AUTHOR

When an individual does karmas (deeds) for the benefit of others, the intrinsic rewards are greater than when you do them for yourself. My mission in writing Touchdown is to share my knowledge, skills, and experience with my fellow salespersons and anyone who wants to be the number one salesperson in his or her organization. I will navigate the readers through all the important phases of selling and help them to become professional salespersons. Hence, you will achieve your sales goals by executing eight key factors to score touchdowns in selling. This book will guide you in your quest to improve revenues, increase profits, and create wealth both for yourself and for your company,

I sincerely want to share my success in selling with millions of my readers in the USA and around the world. I hope that Touchdown will help you to achieve a significant success in your sales career.

D.N. Chadha

Website: www.dnchadha.com

TOUCHDOWN 21ST CENTURY BOOK ON SELLING

Touchdown is an interactive and practical 21st Century book on professional selling. This book goes beyond the scope of other books by interlinking strategic selling, team spirit, and customer focus to help you attain profitable sales goals.

Audience: Everyone who is engaged in the professional selling of a product or service in any sector—pharmaceutical, financial, real estate, retail, and the service industry. Everybody is selling something to someone in a subtle way. *Touchdown* can help you sell effectively to your customers and clients.

Eight Key Factors to Score Touchdowns in Selling:

1. Attributes
2. Product Knowledge and Training
3. Customer Focus
4. Selling Skills
5. Goals
6. Plan of Action and Selling Strategies
7. Flawless Execution
8. The Art and Science of Selling Touchdowns

Pay attention to these proven sales mantras:

- Listen to your customers
- Sell with passion
- Have a positive attitude

- Execute flawlessly
- Provide marketing support
- Build enduring relationships

Selling is like professional sport, as it is based on performance.

I am offering you the analogy of Selling & Football. The eight key factors to score a Touchdown in selling also can be applied to the game of football, so this will help you to understand and execute these eight key factors in your selling game.

Factor 1 – Attributes

Positive attitude helps you to sell your products with confidence and passion. Similarly, you have to play football and meet your challenges with upbeat attitude. In addition, the attributes of high enthusiasm and energy, resilience, persistence, diligence, honesty, and hard work are cornerstone to successful selling as well to the game of football to score touchdowns. Football coaches motivate their teams and prepare them mentally and physically to play games of football. It is the high energy, winning attitude, resilence, and hard work that drive the touchdowns both in selling and football.

Factor 2 – Product Knowledge and Sales Training

These are essential elements to sell your products successfully, just as players should have the knowledge and expertise of the game of football. Players also get the coaching to gain knowledge about the rules of the game and practice their skills on a regular basis.

Factor 3 – Customer Focus

There are no sales without customers. In football, we have fans as customers; they buy the tickets, support and cheer their teams and players.

Factor 4 – Selling Skills

Sales representatives are trained in selling skills and product knowledge by the sales training managers and by their sales managers. Sales representatives practice selling skills regularly and they become experts to sell their products. Similarly, football players practice their skills and tactics consistently to score touchdowns.

Factor 5 – Goals

In selling, a salesperson is assigned a specific goal. The salespersons are paid, rewarded, and recognized by meeting and exceeding their goals. Players in football also score field goals and touchdowns. The players receive multimillion dollar contracts based on their track record of success and performance.

Factor 6 – Plan of Action and Selling Strategies

Marketing provides salespeople with key messages, promotional sales aids, competitive edge, and sales campaigns. In addition, marketing develops business plans, selling strategies, and sales campaigns to boost sales. In the game of football, marketing also plays an important role, i.e., media coverage, players, coaches and owners' interviews, and contracts and advertisements by the companies during the games. The players and teams have promotional products and souvenirs that are bought by their fans. The excitement of playoffs and Super Bowls are marketed by multimillion dollar campaigns.

Factor 7 – Flawless Execution (Tactics)

In selling, step-by-step tactics are required for perfect execution to engage key accounts, pre-call planning, routing plans, practice sales presentations, and building enduring business relationships. Likewise, in the game of football, the quarterback and his team score touchdowns by flawless execution of tactics and strategic moves of intercepting, dodging, and blocking the opposing teams or scoring field goals.

Factor 8 – The Art and Science of Selling Touchdowns

Selling is the art of building business relationships with customers with the goal of selling your products and services. Selling also is a science because it executes tactics in its sales process. In the game of football, we also build a bond with the fans and players, and the fans support their teams and players. On the other hand, the game of football also is a science because we observe and do analysis. Coaches, trainers, and players watch videos of their games and the opposing teams to prepare their game plan to score touchdowns.

I am presenting you the preface of the eight key Factors to score touchdown in selling and offering you the analogy between professional selling and the game of professional football. I have pointed out some scenarios in selling are similar to the game of football as following.

Selling & Football

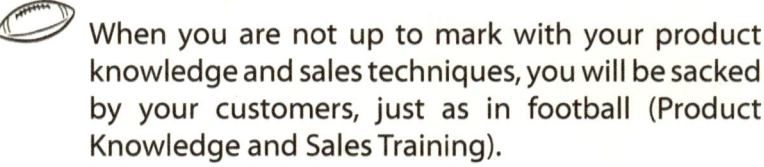 When you are not up to mark with your product knowledge and sales techniques, you will be sacked by your customers, just as in football (Product Knowledge and Sales Training).

If you address customer concerns, you will not fumble (Selling Skills).

If you practice regularly, you will win the selling game (Selling Skills).

If you satisfy customer needs, you have earned the right to close the deal and score a touchdown (Selling Skills).

If you practice together and support your team, your company will be the champion (Flawless Execution).

Top salespersons are like superstars because they possess a diehard attitude to perfect and win their game (The Art and Science of Selling Touchdowns).

Building enduring long-term business relationships with your customers is like scoring extra downs in many playoffs (Flawless Execution).

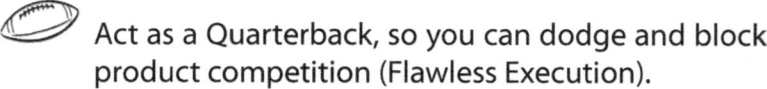 Act as a Quarterback, so you can dodge and block product competition (Flawless Execution).

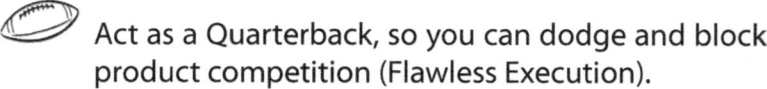 If your customer signals that he is ready, move quickly and score the field goal (Selling Skills).

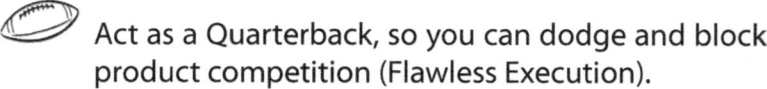 When you fail to follow federal or state regulations, and industry policies, you will get a penalty and be reprimanded (Product Knowledge and Sales Training).

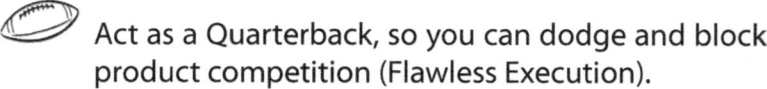 If you do not present your competitive advantages to your customer, you will be intercepted by your competition (Selling Skills).

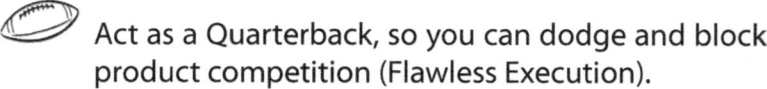 If you are on sales calls, give your best playoff champion performance and get an extra point (Selling Skills).

8 KEY FACTORS TO SCORE A TOUCHDOWN IN SELLING

FACTOR 1-ATTRIBUTES

A positive attitude is the foremost attribute of a number one salesperson and enables him or her to present the products with confidence and passion.

A salesperson confronts obstacles in terms of quality, pricing, and competition. Customers can turn you down for any reason, especially if you do not listen to them or connect with them. However, if you are passionate and positive about your products, your customers will believe and trust you. They will be motivated to buy whatever you are selling. Making a sale is like playing a sport—you are going to win a few, and you are going to lose a few. The typical sales cycle in some deals can be fairly long; for example, a corporate deal to provide medical and life insurance coverage to 2,000 employees may involve several meetings with the head of Human Resources and other key executives. Several roadblocks of pricing, competition, and timeline to close the deal may arise. You have to solve customers' issues and objections to move forward in the sales process with a positive attitude, in spite of all the obstacles that may be presented during your sales calls.

A positive attitude always is important to keep your spirits up. Always remember to give the game your best shot. Beat the challenges with an upbeat attitude.

The second attribute is high enthusiasm and bold energy. When you present your product or idea with infectious passion, your customer will follow wherever you lead.

In this connection, I consider Bob, one of my salespersons from New York, as a true role model. Bob promoted a drug for the treatment of HIV-related pneumonia. As district manager, I joined Bob on one of his sales calls at Cabrini Hospital in New York. His enthusiasm and warmth was evident in the way he greeted and interacted with the office staff and nurses on duty. Even though his product knowledge was not exceptional, he presented his products with energy and passion. He would go the extra mile by arranging support groups for HIV patients and speaker programs for physicians. Bob's success could be measured in tangible terms because we had a fair number of physicians who started prescribing our products based on his marketing and selling skills. So, the hallmark of a good salesperson is one who sells you what you want and leaves you with a smile.

The third attribute of number one salespeople is to be resilient but dogged in pursuit of excellence. You must take your failures as lessons and use them as footprints for future success.

Try to find the reasons why your customers are buying from you and why they are not buying from you. Try to address their concerns and be persistent—follow up with them until you satisfy their needs. Being resilient and accommodating will win them over. When you are starting out in your career, it may be challenging even to set up appointments and meetings. You may have to call a few times before you can get an initial appointment. Gradually, when you have cultivated a business relationship, you will be able to schedule appointments easily, and in many instances you may not need an appointment. You can just show up because of the established comfort level between you and your client.

Amiable personality is the fourth attribute of a salesperson that will score a touchdown. All of us want to be around people who are personable and well-informed.

The best salespersons are ones who treat their clients as close friends and negotiate the best deal for them. If you are in the market for diamonds, you may be willing to buy the most expensive solitaire if the fine points of the "three Cs" – Color, Clarity, and Carrot – explained patiently by an affable and expert salesperson.

Kathy is a top performing real estate broker because she empathizes with her clients' financial and emotional concerns regarding one of life's major decisions. She is patient and understanding and her clients' preferences and goals are always her top priority.

The fifth attribute, one that will pay rich dividends, is a strong and honorable work ethic.

You must work diligently to provide your customers with information, resources, and services. Your success depends on your clients and everyday brings an opportunity to shine every day if you keep them happy. Walter, my colleague, summed it best: "Another day, another dollar." Whether you go to the office or not, you still report to your clients everyday. However, when you are trying to sell your products, it always is best not to rush a sale because of short-term gains. This impatience and dishonesty will always backfire. Customers can instinctively sense impropriety and they will move away from you immediately. You could lose a repeat customer who will not return because he has lost his trust in you and your product

The Checklist of exceptional salespersons who will score a Touchdown:

➢ **confidence**

➢ **passion**

➢ **persistence**

➢ **resilience**

➢ **affability**

➢ **diligence**

➢ **honesty**

These attributes always crack the code of success. Whenever you go in for a sales call, keep this checklist in mind. These attributes are essential elements to score a Touchdown in selling. You may have seen that coaches always have a pep talk to motivate their teams before their practice sessions, playoffs, and championship games. They want their players to play the games with a winning attitude, passion and do their best performance.Similarly; you have to sell your products with confidence, passion and with a winning attitude in order to achieve your sales goals.

There are three important phases of selling:

1. Attributes

2. Acquiring product knowledge, customers focus, selling skills, plan of action, and marketing plans.

3. Seamless Execution and Assessments

I shall navigate you through all the three phases of selling to Score Touchdowns in Selling in the subsequent chapters.

FACTOR 2-PRODUCT KNOWLEDGE & SALES TRAINING

When a company hires you as a professional sales representative, you are required to undergo training. The training may include studying the company's

- ➢ Mission statement
- ➢ Policies and procedures
- ➢ Benefits
- ➢ Product information
- ➢ Marketing trends
- ➢ Sales strategies
- ➢ Annual revenues

Your manager will explain your job responsibilities in terms of your

- ➢ Products
- ➢ Key customers
- ➢ Territory
- ➢ Goals and targets
- ➢ Selling strategies
- ➢ Marketing promotional programs and
- ➢ Allocated resources.

Your manager wants you to succeed because he succeeds only when you succeed. Try to study the roles and responsibilities of the company's key personnel.

They can help answer your questions pertaining to Sales, Marketing, R&D, and Finance etc.

The next important step is to develop an expertise in selling your products. You cannot sell effectively unless you know your products inside out.

This training may include product

- ➢ Features and benefits
- ➢ Pricing strategy
- ➢ Competitive edge and
- ➢ Customer ratings

The IT industry trains sales representatives on its software about its

- ➢ Programs
- ➢ Infrastructure
- ➢ Servers
- ➢ Channel partners,
- ➢ Competition
- ➢ Customers
- ➢ Marketing trends
- ➢ Forecast and
- ➢ Selling strategies

In the pharmaceutical industry training is structured and formal, and every sales representative has to strictly comply with the company code. The newly hired representative has to undergo two to three weeks of home study, and score 80 to 90 percent to pass the tests. Then they are schooled on product pharmacology, packaging, competition, and selling strategies. The training may also include call plans, samples distribution, compliance, management, and electronic recording. These established pharmaceutical companies may have sales training that lasts three to four months. In small sized start-up companies, there may be continuous on-the-job training. In banking, real estate, and finance industries, you are also required to obtain a work related license. Strict compliance to the rules and regulations of the industry is mandatory for all sales personnel.

When you fail to follow federal or state regulations and industry policies, you will get a penalty and be reprimanded.

Initial sales training provides you with basic product knowledge. However, you can gain further expertise by honing your skills during sales meetings and seminars, preceptorship programs, trade shows, and conventions. You can role-play with your manager who can coach you in making effective sales calls. Your excellence in selling depends on your expertise regarding your product, its competitive edge and its rivals in the market. Number one salespersons are well informed and willing to go the extra mile to learn about the latest trends by reading trade journals, by reaching out to their managers and colleagues, and by attending professional seminars. Your training is a constant process which evolves further every time you visit a customer. Expertise builds your confidence which inspires you to score a touchdown every time you sell.

Checklist of key points to consider during sales training:

> Develop close associations with company personnel who can help you answer questions pertaining to Sales, Marketing, R&D, and Finance etc.

> Acquire expertise concerning your products, your competition, and your competitive edge.

> Nurture your relationship with your manager and team members.

> Go the extra mile to learn about the latest trends in your industry.

When you are not up to the mark in product knowledge and sales techniques, you will be sacked by your customers just as in football.

FACTOR 3-CUSTOMER FOCUS

Customer focus is an important factor to achieve excellence in selling. Without customers, there are zero sales. You probably have heard the expressions "the customer is always right" and "the customer is king." In this chapter, we will discuss how we should approach and handle customers in different sales scenarios. Consumers have basic needs for food, clothing, and shelter that must be met. The salesperson does not have to create a need for these types of goods. You can walk into Stop & Shop or Macy's and browse through the products on display. However, you rely on a salesperson to provide specific information and applicable terms of financing. Customers often are well informed about the products they are interested in purchasing, so sales associates need only answer relevant questions and facilitate the purchase. You invariably will see a sign posted in any department store that "customer satisfaction is always guaranteed." They can return unwanted or defective merchandise; it is their right to do so.

Each industry has certain specific sales needs and norms, and ways that selling has to be geared toward a particular consumer niche. Sometimes this can involve distinctive groups classified by age, gender, race, or nationality. IT involves an educated, younger client who evolves quickly and real estate has to be sold with a longer time frame and according to financial constraints of the buyer.

Let me discuss scenarios in which the need for the product is not established and the professional sales representatives have to create an interest and desire in potential customers for his products.

IT industries, with newer microchips editions that come out at regular intervals and new innovative products in the automobile industry, i.e., fuel efficient cars and trucks, create a need and desire to increase sales and market share of company. Pharmaceutical companies launch new products with advances to treat diseases in cardiovascular, neurology, pain management, and delivery systems. The improved and new products will create demand and desire to buy products and services. The financial firms offers new portfolio of stocks, bonds, and investment to their customers.

The sales representative has to use a distinct approach, especially to qualify target customers. This involves person-to-person selling. A real estate client has to be ready, willing, and financially qualified to buy a house. A real estate agent will question them upfront about their price range, location preference, and family size. Real estate agents find new clients through cold calls, walk-ins, and referrals.

In pharmaceutical selling, representatives are assigned a territory and provided with a list of approximately 150–200 potential physicians based on IMS data, which represents prescriptions actually prescribed by a particular physician for their product and their competitors' products. The representative also gets information for the top twenty physicians who are prescribing their products and the competitors' formulations. There is a systematic method for generating a list of key potential customers and physicians.

In IT, or with products relating to defense and energy, you may be selling business to business. When you are selling business to business, you may have limited clients, deal with select decision makers, negotiate contracts, and raise a higher dollar volume per sale in many instances. Your sales cycle in this type of sales is longer.

As a sales representative, you are working in a team with many departments including Marketing, R&D, Legal, and Finance. Similarly, investment banking has a limited clientele. It is essential to find the right match for both parties, carry out due diligence, and ensure that sales deals are in compliance with federal and state regulations. Let us switch to another key topic that is related to our strategy of communicating effectively with our customers, providing resources, and building solid business relationships with our customers to succeed in our business.

"Shut up and listen to your customers, and you will close more sales" is my proven sales mantra.

Listen to your customers, and they will give you all the clues to address their needs, concerns, important issues, objections, and even the timeline to close the deal. Sell with passion and confidence, Execute flawlessly your product knowledge, selling skills, and marketing plans. Provide your customers with marketing support and resources that will build enduring business relationships. This will lead you to the path of successful selling that will allow you to achieve and exceed your sales goals.

The key tips of mantras for successful selling:

> ➤ **Listen to your customers**
> ➤ **Communicate your product information in all its aspects**
> ➤ **Sell with passion and confidence**
> ➤ **Close the deal flawlessly with follow-up sales support**

These specifications will lead you to achieve and even exceed your targeted goals.

I recall one of my salespersons from Chicago. Nancy truly was a model salesperson, who executed the Sales Mantra in her selling practices. She always listened to the customer's needs, concerns, and issues. Her product knowledge was always extremely helpful to the customers. She provided information to the customers and always showed a competitive edge so that they would decide to buy her products. Her customers were comfortable buying from her because she was willing to provide them with resources, respond to their questions, and sell when they were ready to buy. Nancy presented her products with confidence and passion. She achieved her goals and was one of the top performers in my region because she executed the important elements of the Sales Mantra. Later on, I promoted Nancy to the position of District Manager.

Establishing business rapport is an important factor for the development of long-term relationships in your sales territory. I established a wonderful sense of comraderie with the Chief of Urology at a major teaching hospital in Boston. It started with a meeting during which I focused on his specialty and his specific requirements. Then I introduced him to the type of product he was interested in. I developed this relationship further by providing him with appropriate information regarding the efficacy and clinical trials for this particular product. When we had established the necessary comfort level, I suggested that he participate in our Distinguished Speaker Program. As a result, this reputed physician became our product's key promoter and our company's major spokesperson.

Therefore, a crucial factor for successful selling is customer focus which results in increased sales and revenues.

I recall a similar success story that involved Matt, one of the company's top sales specialists nationwide. His secret to success was paying attention to his customers, answering their concerns and issues while exhibiting a great positive attitude. Matt has excellent rapport with his customers and is the number one sales specialist nationwide in his firm.

Checklist of main points to consider while selling to potential customers:

➢ **Develop a list based on the 80/20 rule: 80% of your potential business is created by 20% of your key customers**

➢ **Close the sale by the listening and communicating effectively.**

➢ **Provide follow-up marketing support and resources**

➢ **Build rapport and establish enduring long-term relationships**

FACTOR 4-SELLING SKILLS

So far, we have discussed three important factors for the excellence in selling: attributes product knowledge and sales training, and customers focus. In this chapter, we will review another key factor—selling skills. There are basic selling skills that are the foundation of all selling and can be defined as the Sales Process: Establishing the need, openings, features and benefits, handling objections, issues and concerns, supporting proof sources, trial close and close.

Let me introduce you to your typical sales call. You have scheduled your first appointment with a prospective client to introduce your brand new product. You enter his/her front office and gradually win over his administrative staff by your charming and affable personality. You break the ice and create a friendly atmosphere. Then, you take note of a few personal details like first names and birthdays for future reference. I call it winning the first step – getting through the front door or gatekeepers. This goes a long way and just like kickoff in football. The office staff has invaluable insider information and can help you identify and arrange subsequent meetings with key decision makers. Additional information about the company's mission statement and financial well-being can be obtained from the annual report or their business website. In the initial stage, you are playing reverse psychology – engaging your customers – but not trying to sell. You are laying the groundwork.

It is important to be patient after your first introduction. If you have played your cards right, you will reap the rewards of your efforts. Your clients eventually will buy:

> ➤ when a comfortable working relationship has been established and you have convinced them of the fit between their needs and your products

> ➤ when they want to fulfill that need and consider your product the best in the market

Remember that your customers' needs and concerns are always your priority. Always strive to satisfy their needs and resolve their issues. You sell what the customer wants, not what you want. A successful selling situation is always guided by the customer's agenda, not yours.

When in a face-to-face meeting with your clients:

> ➤ Be punctual and do not waste their time

> ➤ Practice some creative openings for your sales calls

> ➤ Paint a picture: for example, a patient care scenario, if you are selling a pharmaceutical product

> ➤ Open with a close. A particularly effective opening would be "Mr. Smith, my goal today is to demonstrate the benefits of this brand new software. It will allow you to have the latest marketing trends and customer demographics at your fingertips. Would that be of interest to you?"

> ➤ Present a major issue relating to industry. For example, you might point out that small, fuel-efficient cars make economic sense because of the high

increase in oil prices. Then, you would elaborate on your company's energy efficient vehicles.

➢ Bridge from the last call. For example: "Nancy, at our last meeting you had mentioned that you wanted to see our new line of oriental rugs. So, let me give you a preview of our latest catalog."

➢ The objective of the opening is to create immediate interest and to get the customer's attention. Write ten openings for your product, idea, or service and practice delivering your speeches before meeting your client.

Now, you can proceed to the next step—presenting the features and benefits of your product. A feature is a distinctive element or aspect, and a benefit would be something that gives the customer a special advantage or profit.

Keep in mind that a product's special and unique characteristics must be advantageous and lucrative for the customer. Only then will they be piqued by your advertisements and promotional messages.

Benefits: advantage or profits

Keep in mind, the features of the product must be translated into benefits for selling messages to be effectively received by your customer .

Feature	Benefits
Once a day dosing	Better patient compliance
Fat Free Foods	Good for your health and less cholesterol
House located in good neighborhood	less crime, better school system better market appreciation

Write down ten features and benefits of your product, idea, or service. Create a sales pitch that incorporates these features and benefits, and practice your delivery till your presentation is flawless.

 Steps to avoid fumbles in selling:

Clarify: Use questions to better understand your customer's objections or issues and to gather more information and data.

Confirm: Use information and data to confirm that you have handled customer's objections and questions including competition.

Check: Ensure that you have adequately addressed your customer's objections or issues.

Trial close: if the customer continues to have issues or concerns go back to your sales call and address them promptly. If the customer does not have any issues and willing to buy at this stage, go for the Trial close.

Close: Finally, Close if the customer does not have any issues or concerns.

To make sure that you can dispel any customer doubts and concerns: If you address customer concerns, you will not fumble.

➢ Write down ten to fifteen common questions asked in the past

➢ Practice responding to them so that you are comfortable answering them during a sales call

➢ Provide supporting documents, data and third-party sources to convince customers about the validity of your claims and this is exactly like playing safety in football.

Evidence of product efficiency motivates customers to buy. Third-party resources (like data published in major medical journals) are commonly used by pharmaceutical companies to show evidence of product efficacy and safety. Many IT, financial, or other consumer goods companies show industry reports and articles to support their claim. Keep documents, journal articles, newspaper reviews, industry magazines, and reports pertaining to your products and services available at all times. You should review and update this verification data on a regular basis. It should be an integral part of your tool kit. This can be compared to return in football.

Probe or *probing* is another selling skill you have to utilize while handling your customer's concerns and issues. *Probe* means to investigate closely. There are open and closed probes. In an open probe, you pose a question of a wider scope to the customer, i.e. how do you balance your diet to keep physically fit? What is your favorite hobby?

With a closed probe, you want to get a specific answer from your customers. For example, if the customer is concerned about the cost of the product, you might ask, "What is your price range for buying this product or service?"

Smart questioning and probes will help you understand what your customers really want and these may act as line of scrimmage. This interaction will make it easier for you to sell. You cannot move forward in your sales call unless you clearly address all the issues, objections, concerns and needs of your customers otherwise you will drop the ball similar to punt in football.

 Your customers will be ready to buy if:

➢ you are cognizant of their needs

➢ your product and services satisfy those needs

➢ you have addressed their concerns and

➢ you have provided them the supporting evidence

➢ You have presented the competitive edge of your product

If you do not present your competitive advantage of your product to your customer, you will be intercepted by your competition.

At this stage, if your customer signals that he is ready to buy, go for the trial close. This is like scoring a field goal in football. Then clear up any last minute confusion. Finally, if and when your client is able and willing, go for the close swiftly. Get a firm commitment and state the terms of the sale. If your customer signals that he/she is ready, move quickly; you are in the end zone and score a touchdown. So, if you satisfy customer needs, you have earned the right to close the deal and score a touchdown.

This is not always as easy or comfortable as it sounds. Sales managers should zero in on any negatives that may hinder a sales event. There are no excuses for missed opportunities.

One of my qualified sales representatives had an inherent fear of closing. He felt that he was going to turn away his clients if he asked them for an order. If ignored, this hesitation would continue to be a road block in his efforts to achieve optimal sales revenues. I decided to step in and show him the big picture and to chip away at his reservations about obtaining the final order. I accomplished this by convincing him that his revolutionary product should, in fact, be promoted and sold aggressively because it would be of enormous benefit to HIV patients.

It is crucial that you believe in what you are selling. If you have confidence in your product, you will be able to promote it with ease and conviction.

When we require the services of physicians, tax consultants or lawyers, we are charged a fee for services rendered. We consult these professionals because they are experts in their professions. So why not assume the role of an expert consultant and provide the best sales service to our clients? This is a frequent phenomenon in the pharmaceutical industry where top sales specialists educate themselves by reading cutting-edge medical literature; enroll in advanced preceptorship programs, and present evidence-based medicine to target physicians. Consultative selling is not limited to just selling a product. Your industry expertise and honest advice will help you gain consumer trust and confidence. You will raise the bar. Your customers will acknowledge you as an informed well-wisher, not just as someone out to make a quick buck. Educate yourself and extend your knowledge base beyond your products and services. Attend industry conventions that will expand your horizons and increase networking opportunities. Become an industry advocate, not just a product promoter. Develop a long term vision – you grow when the industry grows.

We have talked about selling to individuals; let us move on to selling to groups of consumers. You must acquire proper training to speak to a large set of people. Develop your platform skills. You must acquire proper training in writing and delivering targeted and engaging presentations, especially if you are required to sell corporate accounts. If you develop sharp oral skills, you will be noticed and have a favorable chance to be promoted to an executive sales representative.

Checklist to Practice and Master Selling Skills:

> ➤ **Educate yourself on product features and benefits**
>
> ➤ **Write down and practice ten openings**
>
> ➤ **Probe customer problems and questions**
>
> ➤ **Address consumer issues and concerns**
>
> ➤ **Provide proof sources and verifying data**
>
> ➤ **Answer final objections in trial close**
>
> ➤ **Close the Sale as soon as customer is ready**

Remember to display your championship performance in your sales arena and you will score a touchdown every time. If you are on sales calls, give your best playoff champion performance and score an extra point. If you practice fundamentals of selling regularly, you will be in the end zone and win the selling game. Next you have five practice sessions for selling skills from Monday to Fridays of each week.

Practice Session - Selling Skills

*Please write and verbalize 10 times each selling skill as it applies to your products and services.
*You can also role play your selling skills and sales presentations with your team members and managers.

	10	20	30	40	50	60	70	80	90	100
Establishing Needs										
Openings										
Open and close Probes										
Features & Benefits										
Handling Objections										
Issues and Concerns										
Providing Resources										
Providing Proof Sources										
Asking for the Business										
Trial Close										
Asking for an order										
Agreement/ Commitment										

Touchdown Score : 990-1100 points

Field Goal: 880 points

CLOSING
the Sale

Practice Session - Selling Skills

*Please write and verbalize 10 times each selling skill as it applies to your products and services.
*You can also role play your selling skills and sales presentations with your team members and managers.

	10	20	30	40	50	60	70	80	90	100
Establishing Needs										
Openings										
Open and close Probes										
Features & Benefits										
Handling Objections										
Issues and Concerns										
Providing Resources										
Providing Proof Sources										
Asking for the Business										
Trial Close										
Asking for an order										
Agreement/ Commitment										

CLOSING the Sale

Touchdown Score : 990-1100 points
Field Goal: 880 points

Practice Session - Selling Skills

*Please write and verbalize 10 times each selling skill as it applies to your products and services.
*You can also role play your selling skills and sales presentations with your team members and managers.

	10	20	30	40	50	60	70	80	90	100
Establishing Needs										
Openings										
Open and close Probes										
Features & Benefits										
Handling Objections										
Issues and Concerns										
Providing Resources										
Providing Proof Sources										
Asking for the Business										
Trial Close										
Asking for an order										
Agreement/ Commitment										
CLOSING the Sale										

Touchdown Score : 990-1100 points
Field Goal: 880 points

Practice Session - Selling Skills

*Please write and verbalize 10 times each selling skill as it applies to your products and services.
*You can also role play your selling skills and sales presentations with your team members and managers.

	10	20	30	40	50	60	70	80	90	100
Establishing Needs										
Openings										
Open and close Probes										
Features & Benefits										
Handling Objections										
Issues and Concerns										
Providing Resources										
Providing Proof Sources										
Asking for the Business										
Trial Close										
Asking for an order										

Agreement/
Commitment

CLOSING
the Sale

Touchdown Score : 990-1100 points

Field Goal: 880 points

Practice Session - Selling Skills

*Please write and verbalize 10 times each selling skill as it applies to your products and services.
*You can also role play your selling skills and sales presentations with your team members and managers.

	10	20	30	40	50	60	70	80	90	100
Establishing Needs										
Openings										
Open and close Probes										
Features & Benefits										
Handling Objections										
Issues and Concerns										
Providing Resources										
Providing Proof Sources										
Asking for the Business										
Trial Close										
Asking for an order										
Agreement/ Commitment										
CLOSING the Sale										

Touchdown Score : 990-1100 points
Field Goal: 880 points

FACTOR 5-GOALS

As a Salesperson, you are assigned to a specific territory, and are responsible for its annual dollar or units sales. Your yearly goal is adjusted every quarter or every month depending on your company's evolving business plan. The area of your designated territory is contingent upon the existing sales force and the size of your company. If you work for a large company, your territory is likely to be small; if you work for a small or medium-sized company, your territory may be relatively large. Let us use an example:

Representative: Kathy Williams – Territory: North Boston

Goals for the year 2008/quarterly basis

Period	Product	Goals
Jan. to March	Product X	10,000 units
	Product Y	5000 units
	Product Z	3000 units
April –June	Product X	12,000 units
	Product Y	6000 units
	Product Z	3500 units
July- Sept	Product X	15,000 units
	Product Y	7500 units
	Product Z	4000 units
Sept. - Dec.	Product X	20,000 units
	Product Y	10,000 units
	Product Z	5000 units

In addition, your goals can be based on both achieving the quantitative and qualitative objectives for your territory. You have a goal for increasing your sales in the territory by units or dollar volume.

You have another objective by completing activities for that period. For Example: you must call 8 customers/day, you must arrange 4 lunches or dinner meetings with your customers/week or you should arrange one speaker program /quarter in your territory etc.These key activities lead to achieving the units or dollar volume goals in your territory. This method of setting goals is called Performance Based Management , (PBM).

You can receive weekly or monthly performance evaluation reports. Your manager should provide constructive criticism and discuss strategies that will increase your unit sales and overall revenues. Sales goals can be corporate, regional, district, or territorial. The Vice President of Sales or National Sales Director is responsible for corporate Sales revenues by product. Corporate goals are divided into regional and district goals or quotas. District goals are broken down into territory goals which hinge upon product's history, potential, and marketing opportunity.

Your district and regional managers will receive their bonuses based on district and regional sales revenues. Profits are dependent on dollars generated by teams under their supervision. So, sales managers have a vested interest in star performers who can score repeated downs. They win only when you win.

Corporations, like coaches, should find creative ways to challenge and inspire their sales force to be at the top of their game. Performance incentives can stimulate excellent sales revenues. Another way to spur sales growth and boost morale is to invite motivational speakers and sales champions.

As a salesperson, you can increase your base salary through bonuses, commissions and car allowances. In small or medium-sized companies, you can avail of stock options and profit sharing. If you exceed your sales quotas, you may be rewarded with a sizeable bonus or commission. For example, you may be eligible to receive a quarterly bonus of $10,000 if you meet your goals, and an additional $2,000 for exceeding them by 5 percent. This incentive bonus could be higher in Banking and IT. Some companies may remunerate gifted sales performers by offering cash awards, foreign trips or island cruises. Over achievers who consistently increase business revenues are honored by corporate recognition and lucrative financial packages. They are better positioned than their peers to benefit from annual raises and to be promoted to the next level of management.

Checklist: Essential Steps to win the Selling Game

- ◄ **Assign Territory to Sales Staff**
- ◄ **Define Corporate, Regional, District and Territory Goals**
- ◄ **Encourage Marketing and Sales Teams to Collaborate**
- ◄ **Develop Strategic Plans and Advertising Campaigns**
- ◄ **Provide Constructive Feedback**
- ◄ **Boost Morale by Special Packages and Awards**
- ◄ **Reward by Financial Incentives and Compensation**
- ◄ **Promote Top Revenue Generators**

FACTOR 6-PLAN OF ACTION & SELLING STRATEGIES

To achieve and exceed sales targets and goals, there should be synergy between Marketing and Sales. Both departments should work together to develop optimal marketing strategies and eye-catching sales campaigns. Masterful promoters are ones who can distract, enthrall and capture in a fleeting moment.

The four fundamental of Marketing are products, promotion, price, and placement (or distribution). These functions are translated into action plans and conveyed to Sales for generating profitable revenues. The marketing director, field marketing managers, and product managers may present plan(s) of action every quarter or at National sales meetings.

Checklist: Information Marketing provides to Sales regarding products

* features and benefits
* pricing
* competition
* competitive edge
* target customers
* key messages
* promotional aids
* presentation techniques
* verifying data

Marketing develops business plans with long term vision and selling strategies based on product positioning and competitive edge. It designs Sales aids, which emphasize product features and benefits. It creates promotional messages to pique customer curiosity and attention. In addition, it provides supporting data or studies to back up any sales claims.

Marketing, in collaboration with Legal and Finance departments, also prepares pricing information to negotiate contracts. It provides detailed analysis on market potential and segmentation, target customers and sales forecasting. Marketing researches consumer behavior for effective promotion and makes decisions pertaining to channel policies and distribution.

Sales and Marketing have to be a close-knit team to score the winning touchdown. Both departments are interconnected and interdependent. Marketing provides consumer strategy and advertising materials. In tandem, Sales provides feedback on the efficiency of product management and promotional strategies in the market arena.

However, to provide Marketing with constructive information about product performance and market share, Sales needs to develop specific business plan(s) and a SWOT analysis for its territory. The following format describes a SWOT analysis.

SWOT Analysis

Internal Issues	
Strengths	Weaknesses
Opportunities	Threats
	External Issues

SWOT Analysis is a tool that identifies the Strengths, Weaknesses (internal factors), Opportunities and Threats (external factors) of an organization. Not only does SWOT identify negatives, it also highlights positives, so ideas can be brainstormed to turn weaknesses into strengths. To maximize sales, start by selecting a set of potential customers and develop action plans to turn them into buyers. Plan strategies to handle relevant issues related to their needs and demands. Try to utilize Marketing resources to influence each key client in your set. Finally, coordinate with your manager to satisfy your customers' buying agenda.

Use the 3 Rs to Tackle the Opposing Team

➢ Right target

➢ Right message

➢ Right frequency

Calling on the right customers, delivering sharp product information, and connecting with customers on a timely basis are tried and tested formulae to generate profitable sales. Playing intelligently with your resources and acting swiftly will give you a leg up on your rivals and block the competition.

"Both Marketing and Sales teams need to interact with key Customers and distributors in order to improve their game."

National sales managers often invite marketing teams to work with representatives in different parts of the country. This way product managers gain insight into customers' region-specific needs. Feedback provided by interaction with distributors and conversations with customers are also crucial for product enhancement. Direct knowledge translates into marketing plans geared toward increasing sales in different consumer constituencies.

In sales, as in football, technique is nothing without passion. Versace can organize a stylish fashion show to introduce its new label of designer clothes. The curiosity value generates enthusiasm for the season's latest creations. Gucci will frequently initiate a sales campaign to jump-start sales of their chic handbags or to launch a new classy line in *Vogue*. Panasonic can offer a price reduction for popular consumer items like laptops or ipods before they are outdated by their own latest editions. Usually media outlets such as radio, TV, magazines, trade journals, internet websites and blogs are used to endorse or sponsor advertising campaigns.

You can showcase your latest products at industry Conventions and trade shows. These networking sites are fertile ground for promising leads and future contacts. Both sales and marketing teams meet customers at the company booth to introduce their up-to-date offerings. Supporting client conventions cement business relationships. In addition conventions and trade shows allow you to meet key customers in a relaxed atmosphere: a perfect setting to break the ice and initiate business negotiations.

Checklist: Plan of Action to Score Selling Touchdowns

> ➤ **Work Closely with Marketing Teams**
> ➤ **Develop Territory Business Plan**
> ➤ **Study SWOT Analysis**
> ➤ **Plan Sales Campaigns**
> ➤ **Participate in Conventions and Trade Shows**

FACTOR 7-FLAWLESS EXECUTION

Your company has armed you with its business plan, its marketing strategy and its promotional materials. Now it is time for you to come out to the playing field and shine. All eyes will follow you as you maneuver your way around the sales arena. You are poised to be a sales champion because you have studied your game plan and are ready to dodge your rivals with your arsenal of tactics. A tactic is a device or idea used to implement and execute the sales plan. Strategies are mere words till tactics put them in action. Theories need to be put into practice in the real world. So, tactics have to evolve based on changes in consumer demands and tastes. You need to fine tune your sales machinery to keep up with current market trends, competing brands and economic conditions.

You test your tactics and sharpen your skills by zeroing in on key accounts in your territory. To identify your target customers, follow the eighty–twenty rule: 80% of your business is in 20% of your accounts. Marketing will help you create that critical 20% account list based on market research and/or product consumption.

Checklist: Product Education Defines Selling Tactics

 Throw your passes to the right executives of your corporate departments to learn about different product attributes

Position your product as sales champion by emphasizing its unique and special features

 Act as quarterback, so you can dodge and block product competition

Before you embark on your first sales call, you should be well versed on all aspects of your product. Consult other departments like Marketing, Legal, Finance and Accounting to learn about the different corporate ramifications involved in selling your product. Then ascertain how these features and benefits can be used to publicize your product as being superior to all its rivals in the market. Finally, use that knowledge to subvert your competition and dodge their sales tactics.

Checklist: Tactics Needed To Start the Sales Game

➢ Enhance consumer perception about company image and product benefit

➢ Prepare a routing plan to spend less time and money in traveling and more time and energy in attending sales calls—work smarter not harder

➢ Keep your key customers' business cards handy and review their business developments on a regular basis

➢ Use satisfied customers as reference and request their recommendations to potential business clients

➢ Network and connect with key accounts regularly to keep them interested and engaged

> ➢ Communicate frequently with team members and other sales personnel to exchange and share new and emerging ideas

> ➢ Study action plans of high achievers and learn their winning techniques

You must do pre-call planning before you make a sales call. Ask yourself about the objective of the call; look at the history of the customer's needs and issues that you learned on previous visits. Visualize your call.

Checklist: Pre-call Preparation

> ➢ Collect and organize sales materials like visual aids, supporting documents, pricing information, promotional packages and product samples

> ➢ Practice your presentations for content and execution

> ➢ Recognize where your customer is in the buying cycle.

The buying cycle of consumers proceeds in stages within the sale life span. These stages include product – awareness, interest, trial, satisfaction, and commitment.

Communication skills and presentation tactics are essential to move your consumer from product awareness to final commitment.

Checklist: Criteria Required for Professional Presentation

> ➢ Initiate the sales call with a creative and interesting opening

> ➢ Follow up from the previous sales call

> ➢ Inquire about product usage and related feedback since last meeting

> ➢ Describe product's value added features and benefits in detail

> ➢ State product's potential to make positive contribution to client's work

> ➢ Show awareness of competitive landscape

> ➢ Explain price advantage over rival brands

> ➢ Provide information on channels and outlets of product distribution

> ➢ Prove product superiority over rival brands through verification data

> ➢ Answer questions that arise in discussion to resolve issues/concerns

> ➢ Guarantee viable return policies

> ➢ Write post-call notes for future reference points and presentations

> ➢ Hand over product promotion packages

Your audiences should be participants, not spectators. They should be interested and involved in your presentation. The more exciting and engaging the games, the more enthralled and captivated are the viewers. Our sales mantra says: "Listen to your customers and you will have all the clues necessary to plan your tactics and surmount their worst objections." If the customer is ready and willing to buy, close the deal immediately – don't let the golden opportunity slip away.

Form a connection and bond with your customers to lay the foundation for a trusting long-term relationship. Audiences root for players that fascinate and enthrall them by their proficiency and command of the game. Champions connect with us because of their attractive persona and mesmerizing passion for the game. They attract fans for life. Try to emulate and develop those appealing qualities to captivate your own audiences. Some practical ways to develop rapport with your customers would be to arrange free-flowing informal receptions, industry-specific speaker programs or relaxed dinner meetings.

Top sales representatives in any industry have long-standing relationships with their customers. Pharmaceutical salespersons work constantly to build and maintain business relationships with medical personnel. Insurance, finance, and real estate agents depend on word of mouth publicity. Clients are comfortable working with you if you have established a certain level of trust and comraderie in your relationship.

Building enduring long-term business relationships with your customers is like having extra downs in many playoffs. If you make customer satisfaction your top priority and sell with passion and confidence, your clients will be your fans for the long haul and root for you in every sales game.

Explore opportunities for new customers by thinking outside the box. Scott, one of my sales specialists, was terrific with numbers and mined data for new sales opportunities. Analyze your account history, sales reports, and marketing potential and dissect them to exploit hidden opportunities and untapped markets.

Checklist: Use Technology to Polish Your Game

➤ Study information generated by Customer Relationships Management (CRM). CRM is software that creates tracks and manages sales opportunities. Through CRM, companies provide information about customers' sales data and competition to their representatives. CRM may also provide personalized and group emails sent through your Outlook account.

➤ Examine computer generated sales data for your products on a weekly, monthly and annual basis to help you evaluate the progress of your accounts.

➤ Connect through e-mails and text messaging which facilitate quick and timely communications with clients, team members and managers.

➤ Use GPS to navigate the most efficient way of reaching customer destinations.

WebMD and other such web sites are making sales personnel in the pharmaceutical and other industries obsolete. The physicians now visit these sites to see products information and prescribe accordingly.So, how you deal with the savvy, educated consumer who gets product information/reviews, competing product prices, sales discounts and close outs deals from the net and eBay? Is modern technology a serious threat to the traditional salesperson? Will the machine supercede the "human touch" in the future? Certainly, the advance in technology creates new challenges for the salespersons. But, let us take all these web and technology progress in its proper perspectives.

Technology is an excellent tool to reach out to our customers to sell our products and services. Although, technology helps via internet to offer the information to our customers but we need salespersons to negotiate, offer the terms of the deals, and make our customers feel comfortable to buy our products and services. The customers feel comfortable to buy especially when they know that they can trust their salespersons and have confidence in them. So, the element of human touch and establishing enduring business relationships with the clients is an important fundamental of selling services and goods. Technology will facilitate the selling process but it will never replace the Salesperson. Therefore, Salespersons must embrace the technology and use it for getting information about their products, competitive landscape, sales data, reporting sales calls, and communicating with their team members and customers. Technology helps you to get the information instantly and on your finger tips. However, salespersons have to undergo web based training constantly in their companies. Hence, the recent advances in technology will improve your sales performance to score a Touchdown in Selling.

Role-play with your team members for best sales call preparation. Examine what works and what does not work in terms of selling strategies and messages. In today's corporate environment, we do not succeed as an individual, but we succeed as a team. Share your ideas, experiences, strategies, product knowledge, and competitive landscape with your district, regional and home office teams. **If you practice together and support your team, your company will be the champion.**

I initiated the idea of a journal club with my team members. We started to hold conference calls on every second Tuesday to discuss product clinical reprints and customer concerns. Brainstorming sessions helped find optimal ways of removing obstacles and moving ahead in the sales arena. During the course of a year, our team was rated as one of the best teams in product expertise and sales. We had the number one sales specialist in the country on our team, and we were the number one district in the nation. Teams who practice and play together have the synergy needed to meet and exceed expectations. As we discussed earlier, representatives can receive awards, bonuses, and promotions once they achieve a milestone in their sales position. There are several examples of presidents and CEOs of companies who began their careers as professional sales representatives.

Checklist: How to Collaborate with Team Members to Win

- Share your experience and strategies to ecourage feedback
- Role-play and practice your presentations with your team
- Support your partners' endeavors and celebrate their wins
- Listen to the advice of your managers and coaches
- Enlist help in executing marketing plan if/when needed

In conclusion, we can safely say that it is not difficult to accomplish your sales goals if you work with your sales partners as a team. The selling game is a collaborative effort in which every member's ultimate purpose is the overall benefit and well-being of its business.

Final Checklist: Step-by-Step Tactics Needed for Perfect Execution

- ➤ **Attract and engage key accounts**
- ➤ **Identify new clients by thinking outside the box**
- ➤ **Do pre-call planning**
- ➤ **Use time-saving routing plans**
- ➤ **Visualize and practice presentations to perfection**
- ➤ **Encourage customer participation in all aspects of selling**
- ➤ **Seek advice from managers and key executives**
- ➤ **Support your team and learn from other players**
- ➤ **Build long-term relationships with customers**
- ➤ **Close the deal by using every tactic you have learnt**

FACTOR 8-THE ART AND SCIENCE OF SELLING TOUCHDOWNS

D.N.Chadha defines consummate salesmanship "as part art and part science." Selling is the art of creating enduring customer relationships and the science of tactical execution that culminates in profitable revenues. Factor 8 requires the perfect fusion of the art and science of selling which we have considered separately in Factors 1 to 7.

Selling is the art of creating business relationships with the goal of selling your products and services. This requires the use of persuasive skills and strategic maneuvers to bring consumers over to your side. Nobody will pay attention to you unless your presentation speaks to their needs and desires. You can start of by stressing how the features and benefits of your product can add comfort or value to their lives. Once the initial trust level is created, you can take the extra step and move this client relationship forward. Try to meet your key customers in relaxed social settings. Treat them as friends and learn about their lifestyle and personal interests. Be ethical and honest in your interactions, so you can win their trust and confidence. Arrange informal lunches and leisurely dinners. Let them meet other corporate executives, and arrange seminars to educate them about your latest offerings. Over the long run, these customers will become loyal to you and your product. A social and friendly environment is more conducive to promoting sales than a formal official setting.

Selling is also a science because it executes technological and strategic tactics in its sales process. Pre-call sales preparation should include multidepartmental expertise and knowledge of product manufacturing processes. Sales calls require answering customer questions with reliable and verifiable data to move them forward in the sales cycle. Observation and analyses are the keystones of any scientific inquiry. Similarly, in sales, probing by smart questions, establishing a need for your product, and experimenting with appropriate sales techniques can bring hesitant customers to your side. In the end, the supporting data and cutting-edge research provide the necessary ammunition to close your deal.

In combination, the 8 key factors can create win–win selling situations. By practicing both the creative and tactical aspects in tandem, you can reach the end zone and score a touchdown in your market arena. When you land your first job as a professional sales representative, you are classified as a rookie. Then, you learn the fundamental factors needed to market and sell your product efficiently. You practice and gain experience of selling in your territory. Then, you gradually develop confidence in your abilities which slowly converts into passion for selling your product. This self-assurance translates into increased interpersonal bonding with your clients and special recognition by your manager. It is no surprise that soon you are poised to be the rookie of the year. This is the progression of a professional salesperson who continues to deliver impressive results and master the art of salesmanship.

Top salespersons are like superstars because they possess a die hard attitude to perfect and win their game. If they fail, they try again and again until they succeed. They want to savor the glory of hard won victory. David Ortiz, Tom Brady, Manny Ramirez and Peyton Manning did not achieve their super stardom easily, nor do they take it lightly. Through concerted effort and dedication, you too can become the champion of your sales team.

Checklist: Factors Required for the Art of Selling

Personal Attributes

- ➢ Positive attitude and confidence
- ➢ Passion and high energy
- ➢ Persistence and resilience
- ➢ Affability and patience
- ➢ Diligence and dedication

Customer Focus

- ➢ Acknowledge that customer is King
- ➢ Identify customer needs and wants
- ➢ Follow customer agenda
- ➢ Show how product fits their needs
- ➢ Master presentation skills
- ➢ Provide marketing support
- ➢ Guarantee 100% satisfaction or moneyback
- ➢ Be an industry advocate to gain credibility
- ➢ Attend trade shows and conventions

Checklist: Factors Required for the Science of Selling

Product Knowledge and Training

> ➢ Learn all aspects of your product
> ➢ Identify product's competitive edge
> ➢ Read trade journals and identify latest industry trends

Selling Skills and Sales Process

> ➢ Establish the need of your products and services
> ➢ Present Features and benefits of your products and services
> ➢ Inquire through Probing—open and closed
> ➢ Consider how to handle ten most frequently asked questions
> ➢ Review supporting documents and review industry journals
> ➢ Recognize signs of trial close
> ➢ Close as soon as the customer is ready, willing, and able to buy

Plan of Action and Selling Strategies

> ➢ Follow strategic Business Plan Prepared by Marketing
> ➢ Provide back-up resources to customers by consulting marketing and technical support

Flawless Execution (Tactics)

> ➢ Concentrate on Precall Planning

> ➢ Preempt competition by tactics based on observation and analysis

> ➢ Convince customers of product superiority by latest scientific data

Remember that increasing revenues and profits is an inexact science. It is an amalgam of personality traits and acquired knowledge. You learn by trial and error. Learn from your mistakes and move on. Competence comes with experience. So, use all the resources at your disposal to educate yourself on the art and science involved in making you a master at your game.

Sales Representative's Tracking Scoring Card

	10	20	30	40	50	60	70	80	90	100
Attributes								X	X	X
Product Knowledge								X	X	X
Customer's Focus								X	X	X
Selling Skills								X	X	X
Goals								X	X	X
Plan of Action Selling Strategies								X	X	X
Flawless Execution								X	X	X
Scoring Touchdown								X	X	X

Touchdown Score : 720-800 points
Field Goal: 640 points

SECTION 3-HOW TO SELL DURING THE ECONOMIC DOWNTURN

A seller's greatest personal and professional challenge is to sell in tough economic times with plummeting consumer confidence. The solution to this dilemma is not easy. It requires adjustments to selling styles and marketing strategies.

What causes economic woes and contributes to the financial mire of countries is beyond the scope of our discussion. It could be greed, lack of regulatory policies or excessive payouts to CEOs of failed conglomerates. Another reason could be faulty mortgage policies that cause millions of homes to foreclose. As a result of such financial disasters, consumer confidence is shaken, and new investments are halted. The bottom line is that curtailed family budgets and limited resources turn consumers into close-fisted and risk-averse buyers: the very antithesis of what Sales and Marketing would want to encounter. Thus, it becomes crucial for sellers to change these pessimistic buying patterns through modified strategies and gentle persuasion.

The fundamentals of the eight key factors to successful selling remain the same. We just need to fine tune them like we change the gears of our car when we encounter rocky terrain.

Let us review our mantra to successful selling: Listen to your customers. They will give you the necessary clues to their changing needs and financial constraints. Their main priority at this low time would be economical deals and benign payment plans. To make any inroads in a slow economy, it is imperative that both Marketing and Sales operate at a lower pitch and in a more conservative tone.

This does not mean, however, that we have to ring the bells of gloom and doom. Americans are essentially resilient and tenacious. They have patiently withstood the vicissitudes of past recessions and depressions. They realize that the national economy undergoes cyclical changes but eventually corrects itself. What goes around comes around.

One of the elements that do come around favors the consumer. Ironically, tough economic times tend to create a buyer's market because of a surfeit of unused goods and services. Savvy buyers are quick to downsize and down-market to take advantage of lower prices and attractive payment plans. Discount stores like Wal-Mart, Target, and BJ's reinvent their marketing and promotion plans, discount their products and move their inventory quickly. This tactic can help dynamic businesses survive when other inflexible retailers would likely suffer. It is both plain common sense and shrewd business acumen that both buyers and sellers be resilient and adaptable if they want to maintain their solvent status.

Checklist: Sales Tactics that Require Modification in Slow Markets

- ➢ Approach
- ➢ Style
- ➢ Method
- ➢ Product Positioning
- ➢ Strategies

> ➤ Goals

Let us discuss the elements on our checklist in detail.

Approach

Realize that your price and product value will be defined by your customers. They determine the conditions of the sale, more so now, than at other times. A hurried and desperate sales manner will turn her away, especially when she is already looking for excuses not to spend money. A slow and leisurely sales presentation would be more conducive to a positive response. The consumer may not respond immediately but she will remember you when she is ready to buy. Post-purchase marketing support and guaranteed return policies will be crucial to her buying agenda if she closes a deal. So, try to understand the customer's financial constraints before you customize your presentation. Follow the customer's agenda, not yours. Strengthen your case by stating your product features and competitive edge. Provide information on pricing and payback plans. Accept the fact that it is demand which dictates supply in depressed economic climates. Look for the larger picture and tread lightly. An empathetic and patient approach will definitely yield long-term dividends.

Style

Selling style should be soft in speech and accommodating in nature to move the buying cycle forward. Do not be pushy. Listen to your customers and be sensitive to their needs and concerns. Wait for them to give you the proper cues and signals. While you are waiting, develop and deepen social and personal bonding to keep them interested and engaged. It will be easier for you to close the deal if a level of camaraderie and trust has already been established. Think in terms of long-term business relationships and win–win selling scenarios to create repeat customers. However, remember that you have to be friendly but honest. You will not get a second chance to regain your credibility or your integrity.

Methods

During an economic downturn, companies may have to develop special deals, sales discounts and deferred payment plans to woo key customers. Salespersons should present attractive offers through e-mails and phone calls, promotional brochures, mail-in rebates or through select media outlets.

Product Positioning

Marketing needs to prioritize where necessary (such as in product promotion and advertising) because of budget cuts and slow product demand. There can be layoffs and companies may employ part-time help who do not receive benefits. High unemployment and low consumer confidence means that product positioning and consumer services will be based on pricing, discounts, and deferred payments.

Strategies

Selling strategies and Marketing plans have to be reoriented to suit evolving market conditions. Market research can pinpoint special areas of concern or potential. It can also identify the economic ramifications caused in specific sectors. For example, a slump on Wall Street will lead to risk-averse investors who would rather stay in a holding pattern.

However, people will spend in any economic climate to fulfill basic needs of food and shelter. In tough times, they are obviously attracted to price discounts and easy payment plans; this is especially true of the middle class. Companies should lower their operating costs and pass the savings (in reduced prices) on to consumers. Business entities have to give priority to long-term consumer loyalty over short-term profits.

Goals

You may have to adjust territory goals to meet your sales quotas. Study the latest forecasts for your industry. Necessity is the mother of invention. Rise in gas prices has made the market more receptive to electric and fuel-efficient cars. Alternate sources of energy are being explored and researched. Think outside the box and tap hidden sales potential and unexplored markets. Innovation is sponsored and fostered in depressed economic times when complacency gives way to urgency. Experiment and innovate to upgrade and refine your selling skills. You will not have the time or the will to do it in a booming economy.

Ride out the global economic slowdown. Be positive and believe in yourself. As an individual, you have no control over prevailing national economies. Federal governments around the world are already trying to stabilize housing and stock markets. They are increasing the flow of money to lending institutions so that consumers can get credit for essential goods and services. The American dream is still alive and possible. These are difficult economic times, but they too will pass.

If winter comes, can spring be far behind?

P.B. Shelley

GAME PLAN TO SCORE SELLING TOUCHDOWNS

Personal Attributes

- Be positive and confident
- Display passion and energy
- Show persistence and resilience
- Be affable and personable
- Exhibit diligence and dedication

Product Knowledge and Sales Training

- Master product knowledge
- Be aware of competition
- Sharpen competitive edge
- Read trade journals
- Become an industry advocate

Customer Focus

- Listen to your customer
- Acknowledge that "customer is king"
- Master person-to-person selling
- Learn business-to-business selling
- Customize strategies to suit key customers

Selling Skills

- Establish product need
- Promote product features and benefits

- Handle objections
- Provide proof sources
- Tie up loose ends in trial close
- Close swiftly

Plan of Action and Selling Strategies

- Maintain synergy between sales and marketing
- Study and fine-tune territory business plan
- Do a SWOT analysis
- Float new marketing campaigns to freshen product image
- Attend conventions and tradeshows
- Work closely with Marketing teams
- Accept constructive feedback from manager

Goals

- Meet/exceed territory quotas
- Be familiar with specific regional requirements
- Promote according to area demographics and income levels
- Look for hidden potential and untapped constituencies
- Form enduring bonds with customers for repeat business

Flawless Execution

- Use and adapt appropriate tactics
- Keep key clients engaged throughout the buying cycle

- Be aware of the 80–20 client rule
- Map time-efficient routing plans
- Do precall planning
- Make post-call notes
- Sell with passion and confidence
- Observe and analyze shifting market trends
- Practice and visualize sales presentations

Scoring Touchdowns

You can gain the necessary expertise and experience by following Factors 1 through 7. Then you can strive to achieve the status of the consummate seller by perfecting Factor 8 – the ultimate amalgam of the art and science of selling.

Touchdown

Eight Key Factors to Score a Touchdown
in Selling

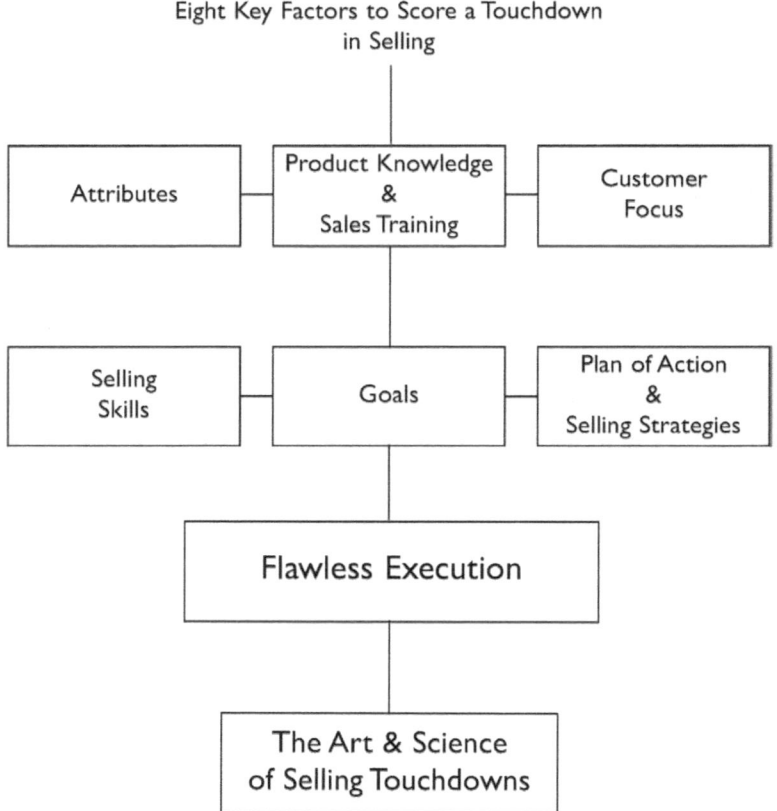

TOUCHDOWN

15 SELLING TOUCHDOWNS PLATINUM RULES

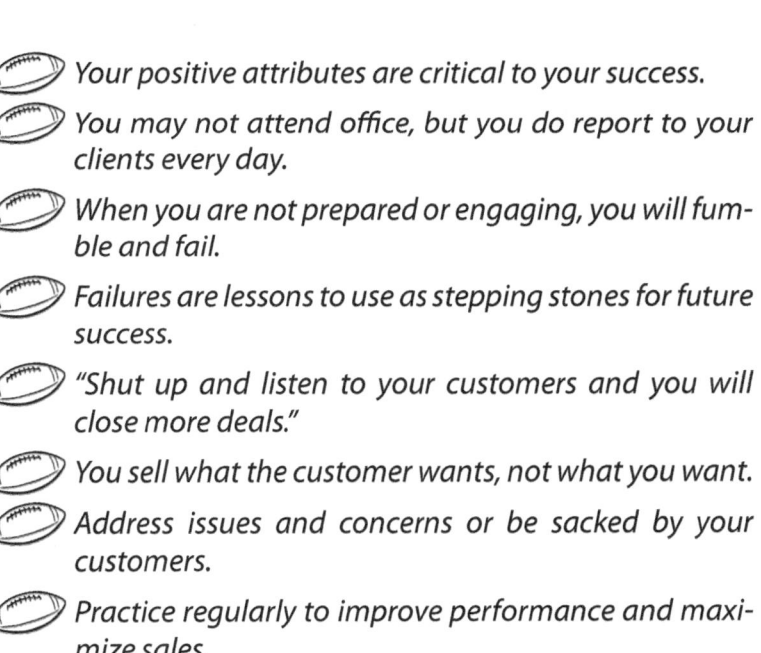

Your positive attributes are critical to your success.

You may not attend office, but you do report to your clients every day.

When you are not prepared or engaging, you will fumble and fail.

Failures are lessons to use as stepping stones for future success.

"Shut up and listen to your customers and you will close more deals."

You sell what the customer wants, not what you want.

Address issues and concerns or be sacked by your customers.

Practice regularly to improve performance and maximize sales.

Act as quarterback for your team to block and dodge competition.

In sales, as in Football, technique is nothing without passion.

Score extra points by developing long-term business relationships.

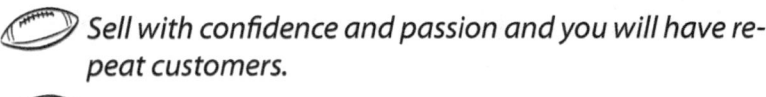 *Sell with confidence and passion and you will have re-peat customers.*

Consider salesmanship as part art and part science.

Have a diehard attitude to win despite all odds.

Perform like a superstar during playoffs or championship games.

SALES MANTRA

Listen to your customers. They will give you all the clues you need to close the deal. Sell with passion and confidence. Execute flawlessly with your arsenal of selling skills and tactics. Master the 8 Factors and claim your mantle of Sales Champion.

ACKNOWLEDGMENTS

My career in selling started in 1963 when I got my first job in pharmaceutical sales with Organon (India) limited. My mentor was Shri R.N.Chadha.I was greatly supported by P.Gupta who was the managing director of the company .I want to thank several individuals, who made a significant difference in my sales career. Walter Schmidt, Tom Browning, Andrew Travers, Jim Boland, Craig Norton, and Grannum Sant M.D

I want to thank Sushil Bhatia PhD, MBA for his expert advice and support. I also want to acknowledge the support of many of my sales associates who have worked with me in several organizations. I want to thank all my customers, who have challenged me to score touchdowns in selling.

Finally, I want to thank my wife Priya, she has always suggested me how to become a better salesperson. My daughters Sabina Chadha and Mona Chadha have raised the bar for this book by their knowledge, expertise and professional experience. I am extremely proud of them and sincerely thank my daughters for their contribution.

I also want to recognize the contribution of the editorial team Lizzie, Margaret, design team, and other team members from CreateSpace and Brooke Holcombe of Booksurge Publishing. I also want to thank Dr.B.M.Singh, former University Senator from Chandigarh, India and Don Phillips for the editorial assistance. I want to thank sincerely Poonam Gupta and Arnold Friedman for their expert advice on the book front and back covers and extraordinary editorial expertise.

My sincere thanks to David Riley of Sir Speedy, Framingham, MA for doing the graphic work for this book.

Successful Selling Stories

(You can write your successful selling stories)

Successful Selling Stories

(You can write your successful selling stories)

Successful Selling Stories

(You can write your successful selling stories)

Successful Selling Stories

(You can write your successful selling stories)

Successful Selling Stories

(You can write your successful selling stories)

Notes - Practice Selling Touchdowns

Notes - Practice Selling Touchdowns

Notes - Practice Selling Touchdowns

Notes - Practice Selling Touchdowns

Notes - Practice Selling Touchdowns

Notes - Practice Selling Touchdowns

Notes - Practice Selling Touchdowns

Notes - Practice Selling Touchdowns

Notes - Practice Selling Touchdowns

Notes - Practice Selling Touchdowns

Notes - Practice Selling Touchdowns

Notes - Practice Selling Touchdowns